Jamonte

Springboard Series

Springboard Series

BOBBI KATZ

ROD-and-REEL TROUBLE

Illustrations by Janet La Salle

Albert Whitman & Company
Chicago

For Don and Phyl, Perry and Lil

Library of Congress Cataloging in Publication Data

Katz, Bobbi.
    Rod-and-reel trouble.

    (Springboard sports series)
    SUMMARY: Lori determines to win the local
fishing contest even though a harrowing accident while
fishing in a creek nearly dashes her hopes.
    [1. Fishing—Fiction. 2. Friendship—Fiction]
I. La Salle, Janet, illus. II. Title.
PZ7.K157Ro   [Fic]   74-3314
ISBN 0-8075-7097-4

Text copyright © 1974 by Bobbi Katz
Illustrations copyright © 1974 by Albert Whitman & Company
Published simultaneously in Canada by
George J. McLeod, Limited, Toronto
Lithographed in U.S.A.   All rights reserved
Second Printing 1977

Contents

1 • Fishing Fever

Pow! The poster seemed to be waiting for Lori to see it. The words jumped at her:

ANNUAL FISHING CONTEST
Saturday, April 27
10 a.m.   Hopkins Pond
PRIZES! PRIZES! PRIZES!
OPEN TO ALL 8-to-14-YEAR-OLDS

Across the bottom it said, "Sponsored by the Chicken Thieves Detectives."

That was the name of a men's club. All the members were interested in hunting and fishing. But some never did either. They all liked to swap hunting and fishing stories.

Hurrah! Lori could hardly believe her eyes!

Every year the Chicken Thieves Detectives held a fishing contest. Every year Lori had spent that morning riding her bike. She'd pedal back and forth past the pond. She'd get more miserable by the minute.

Lori loved to fish. But the contest always had been for "Boys Only."

"Who cares?" she'd say to herself. "Who cares about their dumb old contest?" She'd pedal harder and try not to look. But five minutes later, there she was, back again at Hopkins Pond. She'd pedal slowly, taking it all in.

The pond always looked special on contest days. The weatherman always cooperated with the Chicken Thieves Detectives. Puffs of clouds floated in a blue sky. The water looked clear.

The Chicken Thieves Detectives always strung up bright banners. The banners billowed around the picnic area in front of the pond.

Even the ducks and swans knew it was a special day. They swam back and forth across the pond. They seemed to think they were on parade.

The entire pond was edged with fishermen, or rather fisher-boys. Boys! Boys! Boys!

There were fat boys and thin boys. There were tall boys and short boys. There were boys with curly Afros and even boys with crew cuts.

They all had one thing in common. They all had their fishing lines in the water. They all had a chance to win a prize.

The *Evening News* photographer was always there, too. The winners would have their pictures in the paper.

"I don't care who wins their dumb old contest," Lori would say. But as soon as the *Evening News* came, Lori would grab it. Quickly she'd turn to the sports page.

Last year Ricky Shovan won first prize for the biggest fish. "Beginner's luck," said Lori bitterly. Little Ricky was only eight. But there he was in the newspaper, smiling at her.

Wasn't Lori the one who had shown him how to fish? Wasn't she always helping him untangle his line? Didn't she teach him how to unhook a catfish? That was tricky. Catfish have sharp fins.

"It's just not fair," Lori had complained later to Chris Hodge.

Chris was two grades ahead of Lori in school. He liked fishing with her. His friends teased him about it, but he didn't care.

Lori Davis was a quiet and patient fishing buddy. She didn't make a racket and scare the fish. She knew where to find the juiciest night crawlers. She didn't mind loaning a guy a fish-hook. She always remembered to bring her pocketknife.

"Look, Lori," Chris had said. "Ever since I've been eight, I've been trying to win. I haven't won a prize yet. It's mostly luck, I guess. Really, you're not missing much."

"I guess you're right," Lori had said. But all she could see was Ricky's face. Now, a year later, she still saw him smiling up from the newspaper.

This year things would be different. "Open to all 8-to-14-year-olds," Lori said over to herself. The poster didn't say "Boys Only" this time.

Every day Lori went by Clark's Grocery Store. The two first prizes were in the window.

The prize for catching the most fish was a tackle box. The lid was open to show the contents. There were shiny silver fishhooks and feathered lures. There was a fish scaler. There was even a roll of nylon line.

But Lori never spent much time looking at the tackle box. She didn't waste time on the prize for catching the smallest fish either. It was wrapped in white paper with a red ribbon. Lori never spent a second wondering about what was inside.

The prize for catching the largest fish was a spinning rod. Lori could hardly take her eyes off it. What a beauty!

The rod was tapered hardwood. The handgrip was cork. Lori could almost feel it in her hand. The reel was an open one. It would be a cinch to use.

Lori closed her eyes. She pressed her forehead against the window. She imagined she was casting. The line would land halfway across the pond. Immediately the bobber would start to dance. A bite! She'd reel in carefully.

Sometimes she'd pretend to land a large bass. Sometimes it would be a mackerel. She even pretended to catch trout in mountain streams.

Once Chris caught her dreaming in front of the store window. "Hey, Lori, are you sick or something?" he asked. Lori opened her eyes. She was back on Main Street. The wonderful spinning rod was back in Clark's window.

"No, I'm OK," she said.

"Wow! They really picked a rod this year," Chris said. He looked at the rod and whistled softly. "I guess this is my last chance for it. I'm fourteen now, you know. But I'm not counting on winning. Not with my luck."

Lori looked at Chris. She hadn't thought about anyone else winning. This would be Chris's sixth try for the prize. It would be his last chance. Still, Lori wanted that rod.

"Hey, how about helping me with my paper route?" Chris asked. "Then we'll have time to go to the creek. The trout are really jumping."

"It's a deal!" said Lori. She felt like giving Chris a kiss or something. Of course she never would. He'd hate it. She really loved trout fishing. She kind of loved Chris for taking her.

The creek was dangerous. Its banks were steep. The water ran swiftly at this time of year. The stones were smooth and slippery. It was easy to fall.

ANNUAL FISHING
CONTEST
SATURDAY, APRIL 27
10 a.m. HOPKINS POND

VALUABLE PRIZES

Lori could fish at Hopkins Pond by herself. But the creek was something else. The creek was out of bounds for her. She could only go there with a grown-up. But wasn't Chris almost a grown-up?

Lori and Chris divided the newspapers.

"You remember the route, don't you?" Chris asked.

"Sure," said Lori. "Come on, Chris. Trout's a-wasting!"

Chris laughed. "OK, you take Main Street, Oak, and that section. Then get your gear and meet me back here by four."

"Don't forget your socks," Lori called.

Lori and Chris wore rubber hip boots for trout fishing. But boots weren't enough. The water was so cold that they needed extra warm socks. Chris was an expert at forgetting his.

Lori was good at delivering papers. She folded them a special way. Whack! She tossed each newspaper on the customer's doorstep. She was soon finished.

Lori rushed home and pulled on her blue jeans. "Going fishing, Mom," she hollered.

Her mother spotted Lori's hip boots. They meant fishing in the creek, not the pond.

"Fishing where and with whom?" her mother asked.

"Down at the creek with Chris," Lori answered, and held her breath.

"Chris and who else?" her mother asked.

Oh, wow! Would her mother never stop treating her like a baby?

"Chris's fourteen, Mom. Please, can't I go? He's waiting. I'm late."

"All right, this time," her mother said. "But next time ask me before you make plans. And Lori," Mrs. Davis added, "don't lose track of the time. Dad shouldn't have to chase you home for dinner."

"Sure, Mom. I'll even catch some trout for dinner," Lori said.

"I'm cooking spaghetti and meatballs, in case you don't. Now you be careful down there."

But Lori didn't hear. She tossed her boots and tackle box in the basket of her bike. Carefully balancing her rod, she rode over to Clark's store.

2 • Hip Boots

Chris and Lori arrived at the store at the same time. Together they rode down to the creek.

Chris scrambled down the steep slope. Lori followed. They stood together at the edge of the creek.

There was a special feeling of aloneness. The rushing water drowned out all other sounds. They could not even hear the highway traffic.

It was a weekday. No one else was fishing. Lori and Chris smiled at each other. Was anything in the world better than fishing?

Quickly the two pulled off their sneakers. "Oh, shoot!" said Lori. "This time *I* forgot my warm socks."

"OK, Miss Smarty," said Chris. "This time you'll have the cold toes."

Chris took a ragged lure from his tackle box. He cast his line and waded into the water.

Lori opened her tackle box. She looked over her lures. She'd try to land a fish from shore.

Which lure would tempt a trout? She fingered her old lures. They looked shabby next to a new one she'd been saving. It had bright blue and red feathers. What fish could resist it?

Lori hooked the new lure on her line and cast. Within seconds there was a pull. She forgot her resolution to stay out of the water. Carefully she waded into the middle of the stream.

She played the trout's own game. She tightened and slackened the line. When the fish slowed down, she reeled him in. The trout was pulling now, fighting for its life. It grew harder to turn the reel. Lori's arms ached with the effort.

"Stay with it, Lori," Chris shouted over the roaring waters.

Lori turned the reel with all her might. There it was! A beauty! It was the biggest fish she'd ever hooked!

Seeing the fish seemed to give Lori new energy. Quickly and expertly she tightened the last length of line.

Before she knew it, she was standing on the shore, holding the trout.

"Good going," said Chris, wading over to her. He carefully removed the lure from the fish's mouth. Lori opened a link on her metal chain. Chris slipped the fish on the chain. He looped the top link around a thin stump. The fish dangled in the water.

The trout was a real rainbow. Its sleek body was like trapped sunlight. It was the most beautiful thing Lori had ever seen.

"Chris," Lori asked, "can I say something dumb, real dumb?"

"Well, if it's not too dumb," Chris said. He grinned to himself. What a funny little kid she was.

"You know something crazy? I really love that fish," she said. "I really love it."

"I think I know what you mean," Chris said. He did. There is a special something between a fisherman and a fish.

"Hey," he said. "You must be freezing. Your teeth are chattering."

Lori was cold. She swung her arms and shook her legs. That would warm her up.

"Can I try your lucky lure?" Chris asked.

"Sure," said Lori.

She watched Chris prepare to cast. She hooked an old lure on her line. It would be nice to catch another trout. But she'd be happy enough with the one she caught.

Chris started to wade back into the stream. "Hey, look, Lori," he shouted. "A water snake!"

Still holding his rod, Chris started to follow the snake.

"Yuk," said Lori to herself. There was one thing she didn't like about Chris. Snakes. He was fascinated by them. He'd catch one, study it, and let it go.

Lori wasn't afraid of snakes. She just didn't like them.

In the early spring, snakes are slower. They're easier to catch.

"I got it!" shouted Chris. He leaned over. Splash! He fell into the water.

At first Lori laughed. "Serves you right!" she said. But Chris wasn't getting up.

"Chris! Stop fooling!" she shouted. Without reeling in her line she waded into the water.

Chris's head was halfway under water. The water was turning red.

Lori threw down her rod. She tried to drag Chris up. But his limp body was too heavy for her. The best she could do was squat in the water. Then she could prop Chris's head against her knees.

Lori gulped when she lifted his head. Chris must have hit his head against a rock. There was a big gash on his forehead. Blood was spurting out. She felt sick.

"Help! Help!" she screamed. But she knew that no one could hear her.

The rushing water drowned out all other sound. She tried to move Chris again. His eyes were closed. Should she go for help? How could she? She didn't dare leave him in the water.

Lori pressed her palm against the wound. She pressed as hard as she could. The blood felt warm against her cold hand.

She watched the current carry her rod downstream. It didn't seem very important.

Little by little the bleeding slowed. Lori was freezing. Her legs felt numb.

Chris's eyes flickered open and shut. He didn't seem to see her.

If only Chris wasn't crazy about snakes. If

only other fishermen were there. If only. If only . . .

Chris's head seemed to weigh a ton. How long could she support it?

A million years passed before Lori heard the voice. "Lori! Lori!" shouted her father.

Lori tried to call back over the churning water. She could hardly move her lips. Twilight had started in the shaded glen. Her father was turning, going upstream.

"Dad!" she screamed with all her might.

Her father turned. He ran along the bank. "Lori, get out of there! Are you hurt? Can't you move?" he called.

"It's Chris. He's hurt bad. I can't let go."

Her father waded into the stream, shoes and all. He took one look at Chris and said, "We need help, Lori. I'll have to get it. Can you hold on a little longer?"

Lori nodded. She felt as if all her strength was gone. She couldn't move her legs. She wished Dad would pick her up. She wanted to be cuddled in his strong arms. She wanted to forget about everything else. But she couldn't.

Her father pulled off his jacket. He spread it over her shoulders. It slipped into the water.

He tore two long strips from one of his shirt sleeves. "Take your hand away," he ordered.

Lori could hardly move her hand. It felt numb. Her father knelt in the water. He folded one strip into a square. He pressed it against Chris's cut.

"Hold this steady," he said.

Lori couldn't. She didn't think she could make her body do one more thing.

"Come on now. Don't let a fish go when it's caught."

Lori forced herself. She held the square. Her father quickly wrapped the other strip around Chris's head. He lifted the boy out of the water.

"Can you walk?" her father asked Lori.

Lori tried to stand. Her cramped legs wouldn't move. She couldn't even tell him.

"You've got to hold on a little longer," her father said. "Let me get Chris ashore. I'll go for help."

Lori nodded. She felt lightheaded, not so cold anymore. She could wait.

Her father waded to the shore. He lowered Chris to the bank of the creek. He hesitated a moment. What should he do next? He started up the steep slope. Something made him turn back. He waded into the creek again.

Lori was slumped in the water, half conscious. Her father lifted her and carried her dripping to the shore.

"Stay awake, Lori," her father pleaded as he rubbed her cold face and hands. "You have to stay awake. I have to get help. Keep talking to Chris. Keep talking."

A little color returned to Lori's face. "I'll try," she said almost soundlessly.

Her father climbed the slope. It was growing dark quickly. He ran to his car. He threw on the emergency flashers. He found a flashlight in the glove compartment. There was an old blanket in the trunk.

Within seconds a truck pulled over. It was a tow truck from Maroney's Garage.

"Got motor trouble, mister?" the driver asked.

"Kid trouble. Serious," Lori's father said.

24

"Here, take my jacket," said the driver. "I'll use my two-way radio to get an ambulance."

Lori's father hurried back to Lori and Chris. He wrapped Chris in the blanket. He wrapped Lori in the truck driver's jacket.

He pulled off their hip boots. The ambulance siren wailed over the sound of rushing water.

"My trout. My trout," mumbled Lori. The ambulance crew lifted her onto a stretcher. "My trout," she repeated.

Chris wasn't talking. His eyes were closed.

The ambulance rushed the two friends to the hospital. By the time they arrived, they both were conscious.

3 • Lucky Kids

The emergency room of the hospital was full of strange gadgets and bright lights.

A friendly nurse hustled Lori out of her wet clothes and helped her into a short white nightie. "We call these 'fanny freezers'," the nurse explained as she bundled Lori in several layers of warm blankets.

Lori thought that was a perfect name. The gown tied behind her neck, but the back was open.

"I sure wouldn't want to go fishing in this thing," Lori said.

"Don't try it," said the nurse with a laugh.

"What's happening to Chris?" Lori asked.

"First the hospital called his parents. Right now he's in X ray having his picture taken. Once the doctor is sure that there is no serious damage he'll sew up that cut."

"You mean with a needle and thread? Ouch! That's going to hurt," Lori said.

"Not really," answered the nurse. "We'll give him something so he won't feel a thing. Now you make a fist so that I can take your blood pressure."

After that the nurse wheeled Lori into the hall. "I'll stay with you until your bed is ready," she said.

Soon Lori could hear voices. The doctor was talking to her parents. Chris's folks were there, too.

"You're going to have two weak kids for a few days," the doctor said. "They're both in slight shock from the cold. Chris had a nasty gash. Luckily it just missed an important artery. He's all stitched up now."

"Things could be a lot worse," said Mr. Hodge.

"That Lori is a spunky little girl," the doctor

went on. "Chris could have died if she wasn't. We'll keep both kids here overnight. You can visit them in a few minutes."

"Oh, wow!" said Lori to the nurse, who wheeled her onto the elevator. "I'm going to catch it for sure!"

But when Lori's parents arrived at her room, they just hugged her.

"We're very proud of you," they said.

Chris's parents both shook her hand and thanked her. "We don't want to think of what could have happened," his mother said. "If Chris had gone fishing alone . . ."

"Fishing—fish!" said Lori. "My trout! My beautiful trout! Did you bring it?"

"Bring what?" asked her father.

"I caught this trout, a real beauty. Two feet long. It's on my chain down by the creek. I have to get it. I just *have* to!"

"Not now you don't," said her mother firmly.

"But, Mom," Lori pleaded. "It's the most beautiful fish in the world."

"Two feet long, eh?" said her father. "You sound like one of the Chicken Thieves Detectives yourself. I tell you what. First thing tomorrow I'll look for it. If it's half as big as you say, the newspaper might even be interested."

"Thanks, Dad," Lori said. "Thanks a million! Wait till you see it. Just wait!"

Chris's parents went on to see him. Lori's parents left. Full of warm soup and with a hot water bottle tucked under her feet, Lori soon fell asleep.

The next morning the doctor said Lori and Chris could both go home. He left orders for

their parents. Lori would have to spend the rest of the day in bed. Chris would have to stay home an extra day.

Chris's mother brought Lori and Chris clean clothes to wear home. Just as they were going out the door of the hospital someone else was coming in. It was Mark Martin, the newspaper photographer.

Snap! Mark Martin took Lori's picture. Click! He took Chris's picture. Snap! Click! He took pictures of them together.

"These kids are hot news, Mrs. Hodge," the photographer explained. "You've got to let me ask them some questions." He persuaded Mrs. Hodge to let him treat Lori and Chris to milk-shakes at the hospital cafeteria.

Lori had to answer most of the questions. Chris didn't remember much after his fall.

"Thanks. I better run now," said Mark Martin. "The paper goes to press at noon."

Chris looked at Lori. What can you say to someone who saved your life? "Want to see my stitches?" Chris asked.

"Sure," said Lori.

Chris pulled back the bandage. Little black threads poked out.

"Neat!" said Lori. "You have a moustache on your forehead. I'll call you Whiskers."

Lori twisted her straw around in the glass. "Chris" she said. "Do you suppose this is how it feels?"

"How what feels?" Chris asked.

"Being famous. Getting your picture taken and stuff."

"Yeah. I mean sure. I guess so." Chris reached over and squeezed her bony hand. He didn't care if she was just a kid. She was the best friend any guy could want.

Chris's mother came over to their table.

"We better get going," she said. "Lori's mother is waiting for her."

They drove to Lori's house. Her mother made Lori go straight to bed. Lori thought that was silly. She felt wide awake.

"Dad found your fish. It was still on the chain, and luckily it was still fresh. I cleaned it and put it in the freezer," said Lori's mother.

"Great, Mom. Thanks."

Lori smiled to herself. She remembered the first fish she had ever caught. It was a little sunfish. She had been about five years old. That evening she had slipped the sunfish out of the refrigerator. She put it under her pillow. She couldn't remember what her dreams had been. She only knew they'd been good ones, golden ones.

In the morning, her room had smelled terrible! The little sunfish had lost its color, its magic.

Lori fell asleep. The little sunfish of long ago and yesterday's trout! They danced through bright waters in her dreams.

4 • Bad Deal

When Lori woke up, she felt fine. She lay in bed looking at her room. How nice it was, snug and little. She decided to get dressed.

She couldn't find her old blue jeans. Of course! She had been wearing them yesterday. And her other things—what had happened to them?

Lori rushed downstairs. "Hey, Mom," Lori said, "I can't find my jeans. What about my hip boots? Did Dad bring my rod and tackle box?"

Her mother laughed. "You're full of beans, I see. One thing at a time. We brought your jeans and boots home last night. I don't know about your other stuff."

"I'll bet they were muddy," Lori said.

"Dad brought your chain with the trout still on it home this morning. Then he rushed off to work. Maybe he has the other things. The man from Maroney's garage brought your bike home. We'll have to check with Dad about your fishing gear."

Then Lori remembered. She had thrown her rod down in the creek. Maybe it had been carried to shore. But when she thought of the rushing water she lost hope. The rod had probably been ruined.

But maybe not. Maybe it was usable. The fishing contest was Saturday. It was Thursday already.

"Come. Have some lunch. How about a toasted cheese sandwich? It's after one o'clock," said her mother.

Lori sat at the kitchen table. She watched her mother grill the sandwich. She watched with her eyes. Her mind was someplace else. All she could think about was the fishing contest.

"Mom," she said between bites of her sandwich. "Can I go down to the creek after lunch? I feel fine now. Really perfect. I just have to see if my stuff's there."

"Oh, Lori! Don't you ever learn? The creek's a dangerous place. Dad has told you. I've told you. Yesterday you learned it for yourself. Besides, the doctor said you're to rest today."

Lori felt hot tears pressing against her eyes. She finally had a chance to be in the contest. But how could she be without her gear?

Her mother sensed her unhappiness. "I'll tell you what. If Dad gets home early, we'll both look. In fact, if you really rest this afternoon . . ."

"I can come, too!" Lori finished the sentence. She gave her mother a hug.

But still she was worried. What shape could her rod be in?

Suddenly the doorbell rang. Lori started to run to the door. Then she remembered she was wearing pajamas.

Mrs. Davis went to the door. Lori heard her thanking someone. Then the door closed and her mother handed her a long white box. It was from a flower shop.

Lori wondered if she'd forgotten. Was today

her mother's birthday? Was it her parents' anniversary?

"It's for you," her mother said.

"For me?" Lori was amazed. No one had ever sent *her* flowers.

Inside the box were a dozen red roses. They were tight buds. There were cool greens that smelled like the creek. Lori read the small card in the box. It said, "To Lori. Love and thank you from all the Hodges."

Lori pressed her face gently against the flowers. Yesterday's events came rushing back. The contest wasn't so important. Chris was alive. That's all that really mattered.

She helped her mother arrange the flowers. "I feel like a movie star," she said.

"I bet you do," said her mother. "I feel like a movie star's mother."

Lori spent a pleasant afternoon, studying and snoozing.

The *Evening News* arrived later than usual. Skip Mahan was taking over Chris's route for him. Skip didn't know how to toss the papers. It took him much longer.

The phone started ringing before the paper arrived. Lori's teacher called to say how proud she was. Friends and neighbors called. The best call of all was Sam Clark's. He said she'd out-done the Chicken Thieves Detectives. He was going to propose her for membership. Sam Clark, president of the club, said that!

Finally the paper arrived. Lori couldn't believe her eyes. There was her picture with Chris right on the front page. The headline said "Girl Saves Boy's Life."

The story was continued on page three. There was a picture of her father. He was holding the chain with the trout. Was that her rod in the tall grass? She couldn't tell. She could only hope.

As soon as her father came home, they left for the creek. Lori wished he would drive faster. She was in a hurry.

Lori scrambled down the slope ahead of her parents. She looked in the tall grass. There was Chris's rod, hopelessly broken and tangled. She didn't see any sign of her own rod.

She picked up Chris's rod. It would never catch another fish. Maybe he could save the reel, she thought. She took it with her. Her new lure looked sad and raggedy.

She spotted her tackle box. She had left it open. Someone had probably tipped it over accidentally. She found her knife and a few fishhooks. That was that.

"Bad news?" her father asked.

"Well, my rod's gone. My tackle box is all bashed up. I guess maybe Chris can save his reel," she said. "The contest is this Saturday." Lori kicked at a pebble. "Who cares about that dumb old contest, anyway?"

"Could this be Chris's?" asked her mother. She picked up a muddy tackle box.

"Yeah. That's his," said Lori. "Could we drop his things at his house?"

Chris was happy to see Lori. "I've been going batty. It's so boring—resting and eating—eating and resting. It makes school seem like fun."

"Thanks a million for the roses," said Lori. "I never thought anyone would send me flowers."

"Did you really like them?" Chris said. "It was kind of my mother's idea."

"I loved them. They made me feel like a

movie star," Lori said. "Here's your tackle box and what's left of your rod."

"Wow!" said Chris. "What a mess! Got your knife?"

Lori handed him her pocketknife. He took the reel off the rod. He opened it.

"Well, at least I've got a reel. I can fix this up in no time. Was your rod OK?"

"I couldn't find it," said Lori.

"Bad deal," said Chris. "Now you really have to win that contest Saturday."

"What contest?" said Lori bitterly. "Let the Chicken Thieves Detectives keep their old contest. I can't be in it without a rod."

"Sure you can," Chris said. "Use a drop line. Lots of kids don't use real rods."

"Yeah," said Lori. "Lots of eight-year-olds."

Lori's parents called her from the other room. It was time to go home.

"Can you stop by after school tomorrow?" Chris asked.

"Sure," said Lori. "See you tomorrow, Whiskers."

5 • Have Rod, Will Fish

Lori's feelings went up and down. She couldn't just ask for a new fishing rod. Her birthday was in June. Maybe she'd get one then. But oh, that contest! She really wanted to be part of it.

Everyone in school made a big fuss over her. Even Mr. Evans, the principal, stopped to talk to her. The newspaper story was pinned to the bulletin board.

During lunch, Ricky Shovan came over to her table. "Were you scared, Lori?" he asked.

"A little, I guess. I didn't have too much time to think." Lori was embarrassed. Ricky was just a fourth grader. What would her friends say?

"Going to be in the contest tomorrow?" he asked.

"No, Ricky. I lost my rod. Why don't you go play with your friends?"

"You mean down at the creek?" Ricky asked.

"Yes. Now get lost," Lori said. "Don't bug me."

Ricky looked hurt, but he shuffled off.

"Got a new boyfriend, Lor?" Julie asked. Karen giggled.

Lori knew the best way to stop their teasing. "Yes," she said. "I've fallen madly in love with Ricky. We're getting married right after math."

Her friends laughed and changed the subject. Did Mrs. Levine wear a wig or was that her real hair?

After school, Lori stopped by Chris's house.

"Well, what's new?" Chris asked.

"Nothing much," Lori answered. What could she say to a fourteen-year-old? Her friends and school would seem like baby stuff. It was a funny thing. When they were fishing, they had lots to say. Now Lori couldn't think of anything. Neither could Chris.

"How are you feeling?" she finally asked.

"Much better. The doctor says the stitches can come out on Monday. You won't be able to call me Whiskers for long."

"Well, I better go home," Lori said.

"I'll stop by for you about nine-thirty," Chris said. "We have to register. It's good to get to the pond early. That way we can pick a good spot."

"Chris Hodge, what are you talking about?" Lori boiled with anger. "What are we supposed to fish with?"

"You know what I'm talking about, Miss Smarty. Here," said Chris, "I'll show you what we're going to fish with."

Chris showed her the rods he had made. He had rigged strings to two sticks. On the end of each string was a fishhook.

"You have to be kidding," said Lori. "You're not going to fish with that!"

"Sure I am," said Chris. "It's my last year to be in the contest. It's worth a try."

"You're bats. You're really bats. Only babies fish with sticks and string—drop lines!" Lori couldn't believe Chris was serious.

"Oh, come on. Don't be so stuck up. Winning that contest is luck," Chris insisted.

"Well, good luck. You'll need it. Don't bother coming by for me."

Lori picked up her books. "I'm going home now," she said.

"I'll stop by anyhow," Chris said as she left. "Maybe you'll change your mind."

"Don't count on it," said Lori coldly.

Lori burned with anger as she walked home. What was the matter with Chris? He could make a fool of himself but not her!

As she came closer to home, she saw someone. It was Ricky Shovan. He was sitting on the front steps.

Lori's feelings were so mixed up. She was in no mood for Ricky.

"Hi, Lori," said Ricky. "Your mom said you were at Chris's. I've been waiting for you."

"Ricky get lost. I don't want to see anyone, especially you!" Lori marched past him. His sad face connected with her own sad feelings. She turned around. "I'm sorry, Ricky. I guess I'm in a bad mood."

Ricky's face brightened immediately. "That's OK, Lori. I know you're a sixth-grader and everything. I just stopped by to loan you my rod. I thought maybe I'd show you something about it. It's a complicated rod, you know."

"What?" asked Lori. "What are you talking about?"

"My rod, the one I won last year. Don't you remember? I thought you could use it in the contest. I mean like your rod's lost and everything."

"Ricky! What will you use? I can't just take your rod."

Lori was amazed. Who'd ever think Ricky would do something so nice?

"No. You use it. I'll get it back after the contest, won't I? I don't need a tackle box or a new rod. I'll be in the contest just for fun."

Ricky was making sense. Still, Lori didn't feel right about using his rod. "Thanks a lot," she said. "But I'd feel like a rat."

"But you wouldn't *be* a rat," Ricky insisted. "Come on. Take it. I'll feel like a rat if you don't."

Lori was convinced. What a good kid Ricky

was! "OK," she said. "But what will you use?"

"I'll make a rod," said Ricky. "It's easy. You find a stick and get some string . . .'

"Wait a minute," said Lori. "Don't bother. I have an idea. Just come by for me tomorrow morning. Get here by nine-thirty. OK?"

"Sure," said Ricky. "You mean you don't

mind going to the contest with me? Really?"

"What do you think I am, stuck-up or something? Just don't be late."

"I won't be," said Ricky. "See you!"

"Hey, Ricky," Lori hollered. "Thanks!"

Ricky turned and waved. He was smiling his newspaper smile.

Lori walked into her house. She could hear the squeaky sound of a violin. Her mother was giving a music lesson in the study.

She looked at Ricky's rod. She was really going to use it! She could win first prize with a rod like that for sure!

Quickly she dialed Chris's number.

"You can come by for me tomorrow," she said. "I'll bring bait. You better bring some extra hooks."

"Great," said Chris. "That's my pal! See you tomorrow."

Pals! Ricky and Chris were the greatest! Lori whirled around until she was dizzy. With her head still spinning she went outside.

She started to dig for worms. Even with a rod like Ricky's, you need bait.

6 • A Bite!

Saturday was bright and sunny. Lori was ready by eight. Her stomach was jumping. She could hardly eat breakfast. When would it get to be nine-thirty?

Ricky arrived seconds before Chris. Chris had taken off his bandage.

"You can call Chris Whiskers today," said Lori. "Don't those black stitches look just like whiskers?"

"Don't get smart," said Chris with a smile.

"Whiskers bring fishermen good luck," said Ricky. "Really. That's what my dad says. He always skips shaving when he goes fishing."

"I'll need some luck," said Chris.

"You sure will," said Lori. "I'm using Ricky's rod. He's loaning it to me. He's going to use the drop line you made for me."

"I see," said Chris with a good-natured grin. "So that's why you changed your mind? Pretty smart. Got the bait? Let's get going."

When they got to Hopkins Pond, it was busy. The Chicken Thieves Detectives were hanging up their banners.

Old Ed Cox was taking down the name of everyone who wanted to be in the contest. Lori, Chris, and Ricky waited for their turns.

Ed stopped writing when Lori gave him her name.

"Lori? What kind of name is that?" he asked. "Why you're a girl! What's a girl doing in a fishing contest?"

Lori's heart sank to her sneakers. They couldn't keep her out now, could they?

Chris spoke up. "The posters didn't say anything about just boys. Not this year they didn't."

"What them posters say don't make no difference." The old man was clearly annoyed. "I've been helping to run these contests for years. Fishing is no sissy sport. Fishing is for men. That's why we have this contest for boys!"

"Lori's no sissy," said Ricky. "She taught me how to fish. Didn't you, Lori?"

Lori nodded. She was afraid she might cry if she spoke.

Just then Sam Clark, the club president, came over.

"Lori," he said. "I want to shake your hand. You're a brave fisherman. Mr. Cox, have you met Lori and her friends?"

"Sure have," said Ed Cox. "She's trying to get

in the contest. These boys are sticking up for her. A girl! What's the world coming to? She better go home and play with her dolls."

"Ed, you better start coming to meetings. We voted to open the contest to all kids. And this little girl, well, she's something special. You better hurry and get these kids signed up."

Old Ed Cox frowned and shook his head in disgust. Lori and the boys registered.

"Let's fish over there," said Chris. Several smooth rocks jutted into the pond. It was a good spot.

Chris, Lori, and Ricky each settled on a rock. Lori tried casting with Ricky's rod. It was a dandy. She reeled it in smoothly.

Lori passed around the bait. Across the pond, the starter was raising a flag.

All eyes were on the starter. They knew the moment the starter said "Go fish!" Lori, Chris, and Ricky couldn't hear him, but they saw him whip down the flag.

Immediately lines hit the water. There were quite a few kids using drop lines. Most of them were younger kids.

Lori made a good cast. She didn't have time to look around to see how Chris and Ricky were doing. The bobber on her line began to jerk. She reeled in a fish. It wasn't very big. Quickly she put it on her chain. She baited the hook and cast again. Another fish!

She could hardly believe it. "Even the weeds are biting today," she said. Her chain was filling up with fish.

"Not for me," said Ricky.

Lori felt a twinge of guilt.

"Want your rod back?" she asked.

"No, you keep it." Ricky changed the bait and dropped his line again. He waited.

"Hey! I caught something!" Ricky pulled up his line. A tiny fish was wiggling on it.

"I can put it in a goldfish bowl," Ricky said. "It's just the right size."

Ricky slipped the little fish into his bucket. It was too little to go on a chain.

"At least you're doing better than someone we know," Lori said to Ricky. She reeled in another fish.

"Quiet, you guys," said Chris.

He was leaning over the water. He was pulling the string on his stick. Something was pulling the other way—something strong.

An ugly catfish, a big one! Chris worked to pull it in, holding his breath as he saw the size of the fish.

"Looks like you hooked a winner!" said Ricky.

Lori looked at the fish on her chain. She had a few good-sized fish. Was one of them as big as Chris's catfish? Well, the contest wasn't over yet!

Lori cast again. She cast poorly, and the hook caught on some weeds. While she was untangling it, the signal was given. Time was up. The contest was over.

7 • What a Day!

Kids crowded around the judges' table. The Chicken Thieves Detectives were counting and weighing fish. They wrote down how many fish each contestant had caught and how much the fish weighed.

Everyone in the contest received a gift. It was a package of fishhooks. But who would the three special winners be?

Ed Cox counted Lori's fish. He looked at her and frowned. "You catch all these fish?" he asked. "Did the boys catch them for you?"

"I caught them myself," said Lori. What made the old man so mean?

"How can this be?" he muttered. "You got fifteen fish here."

He weighed a few of the larger fish. He wrote down the weight of the heaviest.

Chris stepped up next with his catfish. The frown on Ed Cox's face disappeared. He smiled as he put the fish on the scale.

"Best so far," said the old man. "Let the girls have quantity. It's quality for us men. That's a fine fish, young man. A fine fish!"

Chris and Lori were too tense to talk. There were more than thirty kids left. They still had to have their fish checked. Some of them had a lot of fish.

"What's this?" Ed Cox asked Ricky as he picked up Ricky's tiny fish. "I won't weigh that. Don't want to break my scale." He laughed at his own joke. "Littlest fish I ever saw!"

Ricky, Chris, and Lori sat on the grass and waited. Ricky couldn't seem to stop talking. He didn't notice that no one was listening.

Finally the judging was over. Everyone crowded around Sam Clark, the president of the Chicken Thieves Detectives.

He cleared his throat. "Did all you kids have fun?" he asked.

"Yes!" roared the crowd.

"Good. Then you don't care who won the prizes?"

There was a current of nervous laughter.

"Yes, we do!" shouted someone.

"I'm going to tell you anyway," said Sam Clark. "Last year, Ricky Shovan had the biggest fish. This year he's a champ again. Ricky, come get your prize."

Everyone cheered. Ricky had caught the smallest fish!

Ricky opened the mystery prize. It was a floppy fisherman's hat. Ricky tried it on. It slipped over his eyes. He looked like a clown. Everyone giggled.

"Guess Ricky better save his hat for a few years," Sam Clark said, giving Ricky a pat on the shoulder.

Ricky took off the hat and grinned. Father's Day was coming in a few weeks. The hat wasn't exactly useless.

Sam Clark was speaking again. "Some people

think girls don't know anything about fishing."

Lori felt her face grow hot. She was biting her lips.

"They should meet Lori Davis. Lori caught the most fish today. Fifteen—"

The kids cheered. The Chicken Thieves Detectives clapped. Old Ed Cox just shook his head.

Lori took the new tackle box. It was molded red plastic. It held everything a fisherman could want. Everything but a rod.

"And now for the biggest prize," said Mr. Clark. "Chris Hodge, will you and your fish come forward?"

Chris edged through the crowd. Kids were slapping his back and shaking his hand.

Before Chris knew it, he was holding the rod. It was even more beautiful than it looked. It felt light and strong.

The crowd started to scatter.

"Don't go yet," Sam Clark called. "The Chicken Thieves Detectives have another prize to give. It's more what you would call an award."

Everyone turned to listen. What was this? The Chicken Thieves Detectives had been giving three prizes for years. They never gave any extra awards.

Sam Clark spoke to the crowd again. "Lori Davis caught the most fish. She won that tackle box fair and square. She didn't win the prize we're giving her now. She *earned* it."

Lori looked at Chris. Her eyes were question marks. Chris shrugged. He didn't know any more than she did.

"Everyone—except maybe Ed Cox here—has read what Lori did. You all saw the *Evening News*. The Chicken Thieves Detectives voted to give her this badge. We're proud to make Lori Davis an honorable Chicken Thieves Detective."

Sam Clark asked Lori to step up, and he pinned the badge on her jacket. Then he asked, "Do you think this will come in handy?" He held out a new spinning rod. Lori couldn't believe it!

Everyone crowded around and congratulated her.

So much was happening so fast—Lori felt as if she was on a runaway merry-go-round. It kept going faster and faster. What would come next?

"Stay put, you three," Sam Clark told Lori, Ricky, and Chris. "The reporter from the *Evening News* should be coming. He'll want your pictures for the paper."

The Chicken Thieves Detectives were taking down their banners. The fishermen were going home.

Lori couldn't just wait around. She'd explode if she did.

"Watch my stuff, will you?" she asked Chris.

She put down the new rod and tackle box. She started to whirl around and around in circles. The pond flew into the sky. The sky fell into the pond. She kept on going. Whirling. Twirling. Around and around!

She didn't stop until she landed on her bottom!

Chris and Ricky laughed. The Chicken Thieves Detectives laughed, too. Even old Ed Cox smiled. She looked funny—funny and very happy.

"Click!" Lori heard Mark Martin snap her picture. The sky returned to its proper place.

"Mr. Martin," begged Lori, "you won't put that in the paper, will you?"

Mark Martin grinned. He winked at Chris.

"You'll have to wait and see," he said. "Let's have all the winners stand together."

Lori, Ricky, and Chris posed together, holding their prizes.

"Say 'reel' now," Mark Martin ordered. He took their picture. He wrote down who won what. He hurried back to the newspaper office.

"Newspapermen have deadlines," Chris explained to Ricky.

"It's better to have a deadline than a drop line!" Lori looked at Chris. Imps danced in her eyes.

"Don't be so sure," said Chris. "Want to go fishing after lunch?"

"Sure," said Lori. "I'll meet you back here. I can't wait to try my rod."

"Can I fish with you guys?" Ricky asked.

"You bet," said Lori.

"Let's go to the creek instead of coming here," Ricky suggested.

"No!" said Lori and Chris in one voice. They

looked at each other and laughed out loud.

The fish weren't doing much biting that afternoon. Maybe they had seen enough bait at the contest.

Ricky lost patience with the fish. He went off to catch tadpoles, while Lori and Chris experimented with their new rods.

Lori's rod worked well. It wasn't as fancy as Chris's rod. It wasn't the rod she'd been dreaming of winning. But it was a real rod, a good rod. It was *her* rod. She wouldn't trade it for anything.

The afternoon passed slowly and peacefully. Lori and Chris didn't talk much. It was good just sharing the quiet of the pond.

Ricky came back with a can full of tadpoles. It was time to go.

On the way home, they met Skip Mahan. He was finishing Chris's paper route. Monday Chris would start delivering again.

"Your picture's in the paper," said Skip.

"How do we look?" asked Ricky.

"Pretty funny," Skip said.

"Oh, no!" Lori said. Did they print that picture of her falling in the grass? She flipped through the pages of the *Evening News* and found the sports page.

The headline read "Fishing Contest Winners." Lori, Chris, and Ricky smiled up from the page. What a relief!

Lori studied the picture. She remembered how angry she had felt last year. She smiled to herself.

"Ricky," she said. "Do you know something? You take a very good picture."

"Me?" asked Ricky.

"Yes," said Lori. "You should be in the newspaper all the time."

"Gee," said Ricky, "thanks, Lori. I never knew that before. I guess you're right. I really do look pretty good. I guess I really do!"